NIGHT, SARAH. SURE YOU DON'T WANT ME TO WALK WITH YA?

THAT GUY AT THE BAR WAS GETTING PRETTY PUSHY.

NAH, THAT IDIOT'S LONG GONE. DID YOU SEE THE LOOK ON HIS FACE WHEN TY GRABBED HIM BY THE ARM? HILARIOUS!

SEEYA TOMORROW.

COUGH

LOOK, JACKASS.

LEARN TO TAKE NO—

HELLO?

PLEASE! I KNOW SOMEONE'S THERE.

JUST... TALK TO ME!

JUST... JUST... TELL ME WHAT YOU WANT, OKAY? I'LL... I'LL DO ANYTHING!

PLEASE! I

TIKT!

THIS HAD BETTER WORK, VETROV.

PATIENCE. SHE WILL COME FOR HER, AND WE WILL HAVE WHAT WE WANT.

PATIENCE?

I'M AFRAID THAT'S A LUXURY NEITHER OF US HAVE.

TODAY...

WOOHOO!

IS THIS YOU HAVING FUN?

ADMIT IT.

YOU'RE HAVING FUN.

I AM.

AREN'T YOU GLAD YOU TOOK A BREAK AFTER ALL THAT DRAMA WITH TYPHON TO COME WITH ME TO THIS BACHELORETTE PARTY?

DRAMA? THAT'S A BIT REDUCTIVE, DON'T YOU THINK? TYPHON STOMPED ACROSS HALF THE COUNTRY."

"THIS STORY TAKES PLACE AFTER 10TH MUSE: ODYSSEY.

YEAH, BUT IT ALL WORKED OUT, AND WE'RE HERE NOW! WHAT COULD GO WRONG?

DID YOU JUST JINX US?

HAHAHA!

YES! WE'RE IN!

AND...

HEY.

WEIRD.

WHAT IS IT?

THERE'S A VIDEO FILE LABELED "LYNX."

I HAVE A BAD FEELING ABOUT THIS, MY THRALL. DO NOT —

THE MORGUE? WHAT?

LYNX.MP4

THEY... THEY MATCH WHEN SARAH AND I MEET FOR DINNER. WHEN WE WENT SHOPPING, TO THE MOVIES...

AND EACH TIME WE TRANSFORMED TO —

OH, $%&#!

WE ARE WITNESSING YOUR FIRST RESURRECTION SINCE ACQUIRING THE TALISMAN."

LYNX.MP4

SEE LYNX #2 FOR THE COMPLETE STORY!

LYNX.MP4

THIS MEANS SOMEONE KNOWS ABOUT US AND WHAT WE CAN DO. COULD THIS BE WHY THEY TOOK SARAH? TO GET TO ME?

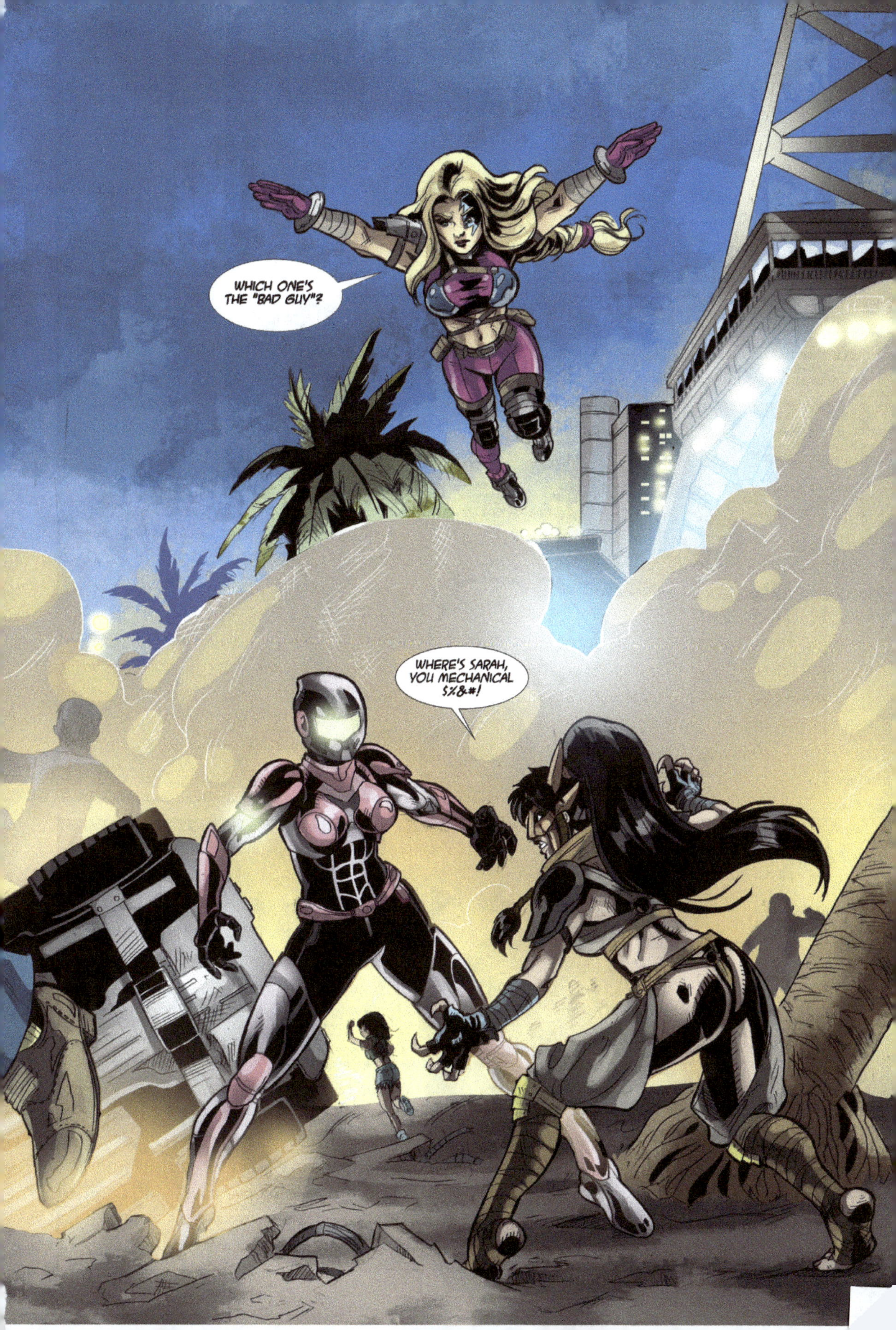
WHICH ONE'S THE "BAD GUY"?
WHERE'S SARAH, YOU MECHANICAL $%&#!

SO. TELL ME ABOUT... WHAT DID YOU CALL HER? VETROV?

COMMANDER ELIZAVETA VETROV WORKED WITH GENERAL MIKHAIL KOZLOV DURING THE VISTULA-ODER OFFENSIVE IN JANUARY 1945.

"VETROV'S FORCES ROLLED INTO POLAND FROM THE EASTERN FRONT, CRUSHING NAZI RESISTANCE.

"THEY DISCOVERED A HIDDEN BUNKER -- A LABORATORY. TWO THINGS WERE INSIDE:

<LOOKS CLEAR.>

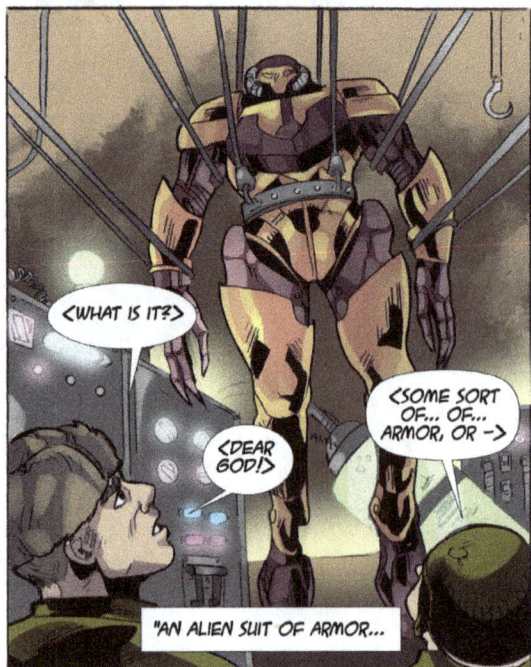

<WHAT IS IT?>

<DEAR GOD!>

<SOME SORT OF... OF... ARMOR, OR ->

"AN ALIEN SUIT OF ARMOR...

"AND THE ALIEN.

"AS FAR AS WE CAN TELL, THE NAZIS DISCOVERED A CRASHED U.F.O. AND WERE USING THE LOCALS IN THEIR EXPERIMENTS -- A NAZI THING TO DO, RIGHT?

<What...?>

"WHEN THE RUSSIANS ATTEMPTED TO FREE THE ALIEN, IT EMITTED AN ENERGY WAVE THAT KILLED ALL THE MEN THE ENERGY TOUCHED FOR REASONS WE STILL DON'T UNDERSTAND.

<COMMANDER VETROV, THERE'S NO GUARANTEE OF SUCCESS THIS TIME. I WORRY THAT YOUR BODY CANNOT TAKE SUCH STRAIN. AGAIN, I URGE CAUTION.>

"TO HARNESS THE POWER, VETROV EXPERIMENTED ON HERSELF, GRAFTING PIECES OF THE ALIEN TECHNOLOGY TO HER BODY.

<YOU CAN'T IMAGINE HOW POWERFUL THE PROCEDURES MAKE ME FEEL, DOCTOR. IT'S LIBERATING!>

"ONE OF OUR OPERATIVES MANAGED TO FREE THE ALIEN AFTER YEARS IN CAPTIVITY. ANGRY THAT ITS TECH WAS USED TO HURT OTHERS, IT STOPPED VETROV — OR SO WE THOUGHT."

"GENERAL KOZLOV RESCUED HER, DISAPPEARING FOR YEARS. AFTER HIS DEATH, WE BELIEVE HIS SON... "INVOLVED" HIMSELF IN THE CASINO BUSINESS. SHE BECAME HIS ENFORCER."

BUT WORD IS THAT HE'S DYING — MAYBE BOTH OF THEM. WE THINK HE SENT VETROV TO RECOVER LYNX'S AMULET.

I'M GOING TO NEED YOU TO STOP THEM FROM TAKING IT.

BWEEE-OOP!
BWEE-OOP!

NOT YOUR DEAD BODY, CRYSTAL, YOUR SIS —

WHAT IS HAPPENING?

OUR PERIMETER ALARMS WERE *COUGH* TRIPPED BY SEVERAL VEHICLES. THEY SURROUND THE ESTATE!

HOW WAS SHE FOLLOWED?

COUGH! THE AMULET, ELIZAVETA!

I WOULDN'T TOUCH THAT IF I WERE YOU.

YOU!

YEAH... ME.

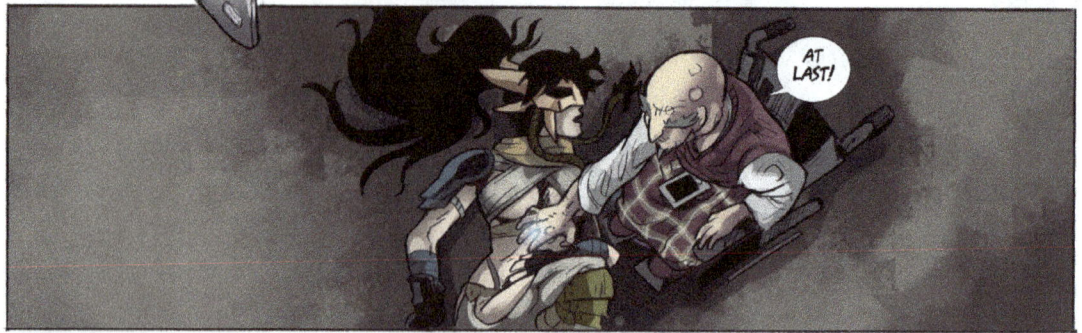

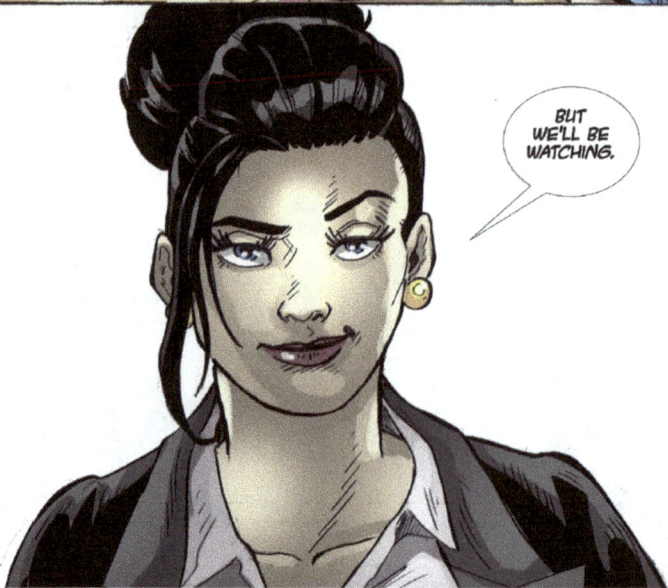

TIDALWAVE
COMICS

Michael Frizell — Writer

Diego Magno — Art

Pablo Martinena — Letters

Alexandre Starling — Colors

Yonami with colors by Ale Starling — Cover

Darren G. Davis
Publisher

Maggie Jessup
Publicity

Susan Ferris
Entertainment Manager

Steven Diggs Jr.
Marketing Manager

TIDALWAVE
PRODUCTIONS

www.ingramcontent.com/pod-product-compliance
Lightning Source LLC
Chambersburg PA
CBHW080537030426
42337CB00023B/4770